ALL WE NEED IT
TODOS LO NECESITAMOS

Learn & Play
Aprende & Juega

Written and Illustrated by
LILLIANA SANCHEZ

Balboa Press books may be ordered through booksellers or by contacting:

Balboa Press
A Division of Hay House
1663 Liberty Drive
Bloomington, IN 47403
www.balboapress.com
1 (877) 407-4847

Because of the dynamic nature of the Internet, any web addresses or links contained in
this book may have changed since publication and may no longer be valid. The views
expressed in this work are solely those of the author and do not necessarily reflect the views
of the publisher, and the publisher hereby disclaims any responsibility for them.

Any people depicted in stock imagery provided by Getty Images are models,
and such images are being used for illustrative purposes only.
Certain stock imagery © Getty Images.

Interior Image Credit: Lilliana Sanchez

ISBN: 978-1-9822-5068-3 (sc)
ISBN: 978-1-9822-5067-6 (e)

Print information available on the last page.

Balboa Press rev. date: 07/08/2020

ALL WE NEED IT

TODOS LO NECESITAMOS

Learn & Play

Aprende & Juega

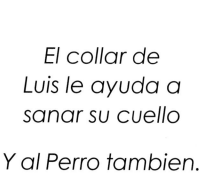

*El collar de
Luis le ayuda a
sanar su cuello*

Y al Perro tambien.

Luis's collar helps
him heal his neck

And the Dog too.

*La protesis de Lily
en su pie le ayuda
a caminar.*

Y al Elefante Tambien

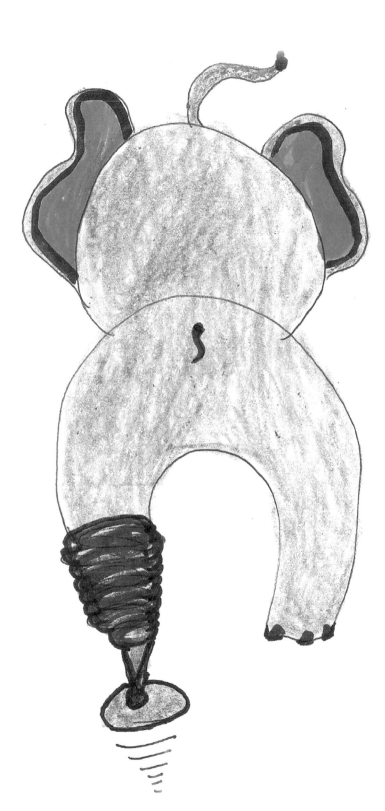

Lily's prosthesis on her foot helps her walk.

And the Elephant too

El caminador de Rossy la ayuda a balancearse.

Y a la Ardilla tambien

Rossy's walker helps her swing.

And the Squirrel too

*La protesis de Edward en
su mano le permite nadar*

Y al Delfin en su cola tambien

Edward's prosthesis on his
hand allows him to swim

And the Dolphin in its tail too

En su silla de
Ruedas Nora
sale a disfrutar
en el jardin.

Y la Tortuga
tambien.

In her wheelchair, Nora goes out
to enjoy the garden.

And the Turtle too.

*Johana con sus lentes
puede apreciar
y disfrutar del
paisaje en carro*

y el Perro tambien.

Johana with her Glasses
can appreciate and enjoy
the scenery by car

and the Dog too.

Con el Caminador
Jhon juega y pasea

Y el Gato tambien

Jhon plays and walks
with the Walker

And the Cat too

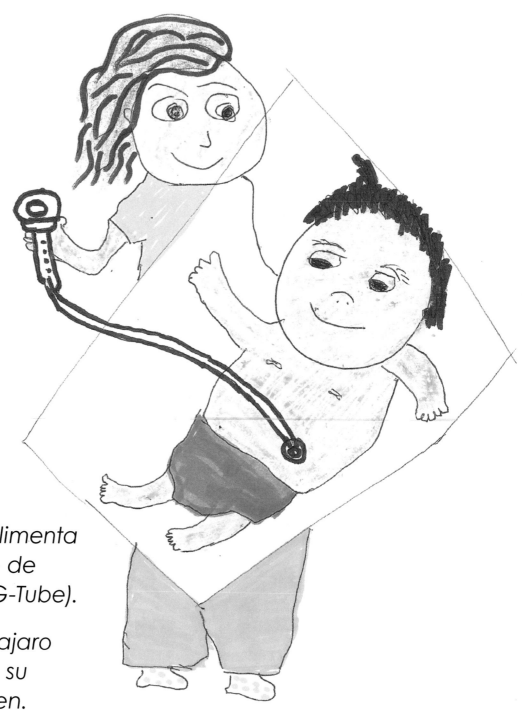

Mi mama me alimenta
por mi Tubo de
Gastrostomia (G-Tube).

Y la mama pajaro
alimenta a su
cria tambien.

My mother feeds me through my
Gastrostomy Tube (G-Tube).

And the mother bird feeds her baby bird too.

Angel camina
mucho mejor
con su Plantilla
en su zapato

y el Caballo
tambien

Angels walks much better
with his Insole in his shoe

And the Horse too

*Ines con su Baston
recorre toda
la escuela*

Y el Perro tambien

Ines with her Cane walks
the entire school

And the Dog too

Beto con su Casco sana
y forma su cabeza

Y el Perro tambien

Beto with his Helmet heals
and shapes his head

And the Dog too

Con sus Muletas
Gwen le ayuda a
que su pie enyesado
no se lastime

y el Gato Tambien

With her Crutches Gwen helps
her plaster foot not to get hurt

And the Cat too

About the Author

Lilliana M. Sanchez es nacida en Colombia America del Sur; de la cuidad de Sabaneta Antioquia. Lilliana llego a los Estados Unidos en 1997. Obtuvo su Licenciatura en Trabajo Social (BSW) en St Augustine College, Chicago, IL en 2005. Ademas fue Especialista de Educacion Infantil para CEDA (CDS) y Directora de Flamboyan Head Start/ St Augustine College, Chicago, 2002-2005 Tras 8 anos de ser Directora Y Educadora en su guarderia My Angels Day Care en Joliet, IL fue que decidio cerrar su guarderia para ser Educadora de Padres/ Visitadora de Hogares desde 2016 con la Agencia de Easterseals Joliet IL Region en el programa de Jump Start Prevencion Temprana.

Desde 2010 ejerce como interprete Bilingue Medica en hospitales e instituciones medicas para ayudar a inmigrantes de habla hispana en sus consultas con limitaciones de expresarse en Ingles. Tambien desde 2018 colabora con el Condado de Grundy, Illinois como Instructora Bilingue de Primeros Auxilios de Salud Mental en los Jovenes de los Estados Unidos impartiendo talleres para las familias con familiares o amistades que pudieran tener desordenes mentales, sintomas de despresion, anxiedad, e intentos fallidos de suicidio en todo el territorio nacional.

Actualmente reside en Joliet, Illinois junto con su esposo Edward Mueller.

Para contactarle por favor escribirle a la siguiente direccion: Lmsanchezauthor@gmail.com

Lilliana M. Sanchez Born in Colombia South America; from the city of Sabaneta Antioquia. Lilliana came to the United States in 1997. She earned her Bachelor of Social Work (BSW) from St Augustine College, Chicago, IL in 2005. In addition she executed the role of Child Development Specialist for CEDA (CDS) and Director of Flamboyan Head Start / St Augustine College, Chicago, 2002-2005. After 8 years of being a Director and Educator at her My Angels Day Care in Joliet, IL she decided to close her day care to be a Parent Educator / Home Visitor since 2016 with Easterseals Joliet IL Region Agency at Jump Start Early Prevention Program.

Since 2010 she has worked as a Bilingual Medical Interpreter in hospitals and medical institutions to help Spanish- speaking immigrants in their consultations with limitations in expressing themselves in English.

Also since 2018 she collaborates with Grundy County, Illinois as a Bilingual Mental Health First Aid Instructor for Youth in the United States, giving workshops for families with relatives or friends who may have mental disorders, symptoms of depression, anxiety, and attempts unsuccessful suicide in the entire national territory.

She currently resides in Joliet, Illinois along with her husband Edward Mueller.

To contact him please write to the following address: Lmsanchezauthor@gmail.com

Printed in the United States
By Bookmasters